ADVENTURES ★ WITH ★
TOAD & WEE

· ·

DREW PERRY

Published by *Our State* magazine, Mann Media, Inc.
PO Box 4552, Greensboro, NC 27404
(800) 948-1409 | ourstate.com
Printed in the United States by R.R. Donnelley

EDITOR: Katie Saintsing
DESIGN DIRECTOR: Claudia Royston
ART DIRECTOR: Jason Chenier
ART COORDINATOR: Hannah Wright
INTERN: Katie Schanze

Library of Congress Control Number: 2016907502

Each month, author Drew Perry writes a column for *Our State*, chronicling his adventures exploring the sights and sounds (and sometimes tastes) of North Carolina with his two young sons — known affectionately in the Perry household as The Toad and The Wee, now ages $5\frac{1}{2}$ and 3. They've listened for echoes near the Nantahala River, driven to the border for a burger, and camped in their own backyard. With the boys' help, Drew discovers the best parts of our state all over again, as if for the first time. The Perrys' adventures are a reminder of how much there is to love about North Carolina — and family.

MAPPING
THE STATE

Good-night words, geography lessons,
and what it means to be "home."

I
t's been a long night. A lot of them are long nights; that's what comes with the territory, if the territory is one boy age 4 and another age 1½. The little one, The Welf — it was The Wolf, but his brother, The Toad, could not at first pronounce it — has drawn a new line in the sand. After he swan-dived off an upstairs bed, and after we got him downstairs and got all the blood cleaned up, and after his lip went fat, and after we counted his teeth and checked his pupils for concussion, we lost him. Literally, I mean. We were standing there talking about how we managed to break the baby, and we lost him. We tried the stairs, the bathroom, checked the back door. We found him — The Toad found him, actually — sitting

atop the dining room table, sorting socks. Or, rather, de-sorting them. The Welf is generally, it might be said, a de-sorter.

Dinner occurs absent any notable tragedy other than food in the hair and a wash of high-decibel noise. We head upstairs for bedtime. The Toad is carrying a book, is bending a corner of it with malice aforethought. "Hey," I say. "Why are you bending your book?"

He stops. Turns. Important to know that almost nothing is out of character for this child. For either of them, really. "Well," he says, "I'm afraid you left me no choice."

THE TOAD. SO NAMED FOR THE NOISES HE MADE AS AN infant, yawning and stretching and straining against the swaddle. No one told me babies made noise apart from wailing. I was still recovering from walking out into that bright Carolina sunshine, trying to adjust to not being in the hospital, trying to adjust to the straightforwardly insane idea that the hospital would actually send you home with your own child. As in, *Thanks for stopping by, this seems to be your baby, best of luck.* So what do you do with a person of whom you're abjectly terrified? Find him a nickname. It's a start.

North America. North Dakota. North Carolina. Trees and sky. Grass and ground. For the past year or more, those have been The Toad's good-night words. We whisper them back and forth after the lights are out. We'll improvise, add more pairs from his day: *Paper airplanes and regular airplanes. Jellyfish and boogie boards.* Whatever fits, whatever seems right. It calms him. Calms me. It's nice to say what happened, where we've been, what we've survived. Like so many things around here, I have no idea how the good-night words got started.

No idea why North Dakota. Of late, right at the end, I've started saying, *Go good places.* We have this thing where he goes places in his sleep, rides car-transporter trucks and blimps and "helicocters" (please don't correct him) off to all the places he knows.

THE NEXT MORNING, OR A COUPLE OF MORNINGS LATER — having these boys means never again understanding the days of the week — The Toad reads the word "native" off the back of the granola box. His mom asks him if he knows what that means. I'm pretty sure he's said "naked," and I try to step in, avert catastrophe, keep the lid on the knowledge of good and evil — but no, it's "native."

"It means you're from somewhere," she tells him. "You're a native of North Carolina."

"I know," he says. "Is that our country?"

So. The globe on the bookshelf. The huge classroom map of the circa-1830 Americas hanging in the den. The atlas. I show him where we go to the beach, and he says, "I can see the water!" But then he wants to know where our house is, and the first thing I think of is this: a huge shaving-cream map of North Carolina in the backyard.

Logistical problems arrive straightaway. I'm not sure if the shaving cream might damage the lawn. Also, owing to a haphazard grooming regime, I don't have any. We pivot, then, to Plan B: Reddi-wip on the kitchen table.

I'm proud of the results. It looks like North Carolina, give or take. We draw in the Outer Banks, add a shaky interstate or two. The Welf starts eating the Sandhills. We locate our house, and The Toad runs his finger through it. It is the stickiest geography lesson in history, but The Toad is half-listening. Here's that cabin we rented last year, I tell him. Here's a river where you can ride in a canoe.

He's getting excited. Maybe it's just the sugar. Or maybe not. He says, "Tomorrow, can we make strawberry lemonade?" I tell him we can. "And will you take me on a seaplane? And a pirate ship? And a red trolley with truck wheels?"

There he is with whipped cream from forehead to chin. There's his brother lathering it onto his knees. And the answer is easy. I've known it since the first day of the first boy. It's maybe the only thing I've known. Yes. Yes, we can go to those places. We can do those things. I have a lot of jobs, I guess, but this seems like one of the biggest ones: Show them where they're from. Where they live. Explain, as best I can, and whenever I can, what we mean when we say "home." **Os**

NC Museum of History

· RALEIGH ·

Explore our state's history at the North Carolina Museum of History, which features artifacts and historical material related to the heritage and experiences of generations of North Carolinians. For more information, call (919) 807-7900, or visit ncmuseumofhistory.org.

FRIED TURKEY DAY

The art of the day trip: Seeking a favorite sandwich in Fayetteville.

Fried turkey on
Texas toast makes
The Toad a happy
day-tripper.

It's something my grandfather would have done for sure. He worshiped at the altar of the day trip. Caves, boat rides, half-obscure museums — and restaurants. There were always restaurants, little edge-of-the-map places he'd heard of or read about. So I know that had he learned of such a thing as Fayetteville's Fried Turkey Sandwich Shop, he would have piled us into his car and driven the two hours, no questions asked.

It would be enough just to go, but there's also this: Thanksgiving was by far my grandfather's favorite holiday. He liked the pomp and circumstance of Thursday night just fine, the meal we dressed up for, the good china and the fancy silver and the carving knife with a name — Bertha — that now rests in my own kitchen drawer. But Friday lunch, a lunch of leftover turkey sandwiches, was where he centered his entire year. He loved the gentler ceremony, the ease of it. That sandwich, built his way: wheat bread, mayonnaise, Durkee Famous Sauce (a mustard-mayo hybrid; go find it right now), lettuce, sliced bird, and a little freshly ground pepper and salt. To round out the meal: a glass of milk and a confoundingly strange square of tomato aspic. As we grandkids got older, we switched out milk for beer. This, I confess, helped with the aspic.

I like the big meals fine, but I'm my grandfather's grandson. Give me a turkey sandwich in the wash of the day after, and I'm a happy man.

TAKING MY KIDS – TWO BOYS, BOTH UNDER THE AGE OF 6 — to an actual restaurant is such a demonstrably bad idea that you'd think I'd learn not to do it again. But to be a parent is, for me, to choose a kind of selective amnesia: I have an unshakable feeling of doom about this, but what the heck? Let's go find out what The Fried Turkey Sandwich Shop is all about.

The restaurant's foremost delight is its lack of pretension: It is what you think it is. You can get your sandwich in a dizzying array of options: turkey with cranberry sauce, turkey with stuffing, turkey with cranberry sauce and stuffing. All this on Texas toast. Gravy on the side. There are other menu options, but listen to me: You have come all this way to The Fried Turkey Sandwich Shop. Unless you are a local and can return tomorrow, you are a special kind of fool not to order the fried turkey sandwich.

The boys were hurricanes. They were boys. I got the little one locked into his high chair and threatened the big one with the taking away of all the Legos for all the days, and I went to get us drinks. When I came back, they were screaming and hitting each other with the table flag. Please, I said to them. Please do not do this. Rise above yourselves.

The food arrived, and I was three or four bites into my Fried Turkey Day (turkey, cranberry sauce, stuffing, gravy) before I realized something was wrong: The boys were silent. I couldn't remember the last time the boys were silent. Here is how to silence them: turkey sandwich, turkey strips, fried okra. Why did no one tell me this? I want to sing to the wonders of downtown Fayetteville, and to the joy of pulling off the road on Fort Bragg to watch the planes take off from Pope Field, but

I was thankful to have been taught to chase after the right things.

I can't, really, because all I remember is that the boys were briefly struck dumb. Or, rather, shot through with awe. They were given the prayer of the turkey sandwich.

MY GRANDFATHER DIED THREE YEARS AGO. HE'D HAVE loved The Fried Turkey Sandwich Shop. It was him I thought of there in that nearly silent parenthesis, the boys chewing and happy and, for the moment, doing each other no lasting harm. It was him I thought of while I ate my own sandwich, nothing like his, and, of course, exactly like it. And it was him I thought of on the drive home, the boys in the back seat, working first through the higher end of the decibel range and then both — both! — falling asleep. A quick sandwich, simple and delicious. Two hundred flattening miles to the Sandhills and back, a handful of them quiet. I was thankful, is what I'm trying to say — thankful to have been taught to chase after the right things. Thankful to have been taught to chase at all. *Os*

The Fried Turkey Sandwich Shop

• FAYETTEVILLE •

For a dining experience that rivals the traditional day-after-Thanksgiving turkey sandwich, head to this restaurant and choose from turkey sandwiches, salads, wraps, and quesadillas. Downtown location: (910) 223-5379; Bingham Drive location: (910) 425-2755, thefriedturkeysandwichshop.com.

A VISIT TO THE STATE LINE

On the wonder of being in two places at once.

You can take a kid
to the state line,
but, fair warning,
he might be more
interested in jumping
in Elk Creek.

Here is who does not care at
all about state lines: young
children. Mine, anyway. As
you cross into North Carolina
on Elk Creek Church Road, there is signage: NORTH
CAROLINA STATE LINE. Beneath that: ALLEGHANY
CO. Another, planted 18 inches away, says, NO
DUMPING ALLOWED. But going the other way, on
the other side, crossing into Virginia? Nothing. Virginia
neither welcomes you nor cares what you leave behind.

On the topic of Elk Creek Church Road: Elk Creek
indeed lies in a ravine below us, and we passed an old
church coming in — but "road" seems a generous word.
Unpaved, steep, barely a lane wide, it's a glorified trail.
Still, let's not get choosy: This is the High Country. Elk
Creek meets the New River within earshot of here.
There's a serious wind working through the trees. It's
either raining or it's about to, and the temperature is
dropping in a kind of sporting way. This is very much
my kind of place, my kind of weekend. I'm delighted.

Or I would be. The Welf, The Wee, whoever he is
this week — not yet 2, he has a mutable nickname — is

eating gravel. His brother, The Toad, bored, keeps jogging toward what his mom wants to call a cliff. She gives me a look, but doesn't say "I told you so." I had a speech ready about my grandfather's love of state lines, about the capriciousness of boundaries and the excellence of being in two places at once. Now I'm just trying to get the kids to stand on the damn line and stay still long enough to take their picture. As to the question of whether it's raining, soon there's not much question. At least we've got a chicken going back at the cabin. Did I mention the cabin? We're on foot. We walk back up the hill to get dry.

A PARTIAL LISTING OF WEEKEND INJURIES INCURRED: The Toad slips on a shed-size boulder, hurts his rear. (I was teaching him rock-climbing. On purpose.) The Toad slips on the cabin deck, splits his face open in two or three non-emergency places. The Wee has a diaper failure — in the woods, on a mountain, in the rain. I burn myself several times trying to light fires in the wind and fog. The Toad gets sent to an especially well-earned time-out — breakfast table; airborne food — and throws a massive, wall-to-wall fit, but pulls it together and returns, seemingly chastened, to the family meal. I tell him I'm proud of him for calming down, for following directions. He looks at me. He blinks. He says, "I accept your apology."

I fell on that boulder, too. I fell right after I told The Toad he'd fallen because he wasn't paying enough attention.

I'D LIKE TO TOE A LINE HERE: THERE'S A SCHOOL OF thought rattling around the parenting world that says if you don't treasure every, every moment of the ongoing insurance fire that can be child husbandry, then you're doing it wrong. And, yes, my heart is larger, post-Toad and again post-Wee, than I ever thought it could be. But, y'all: Each night, once we've gotten them feetsuited and face-washed and snuggled down with the correct stuffed animals, my wife and I tiptoe out to the cabin's wrap-around deck. Below us, the New River shines even under cloud cover, tucks briefly back into North Carolina. The fire in the firepit is down to coals. The s'mores stuff

It's plenty excellent to be in both places, both lives, at once.

is put away. There's not a single rocks glass in any cabinet, so we're drinking from coffee cups, which work just fine. We toast the dog, who lived to be 17, whose ashes are scattered here. We toast our old lives. We toast our new ones, also, but these moments — when the Tilt-A-Whirl slows, opens our nights back up just a little — we treasure these, too.

Sunday morning, The Toad wants to go see Elk Creek. We drive down there; we do not stop at the state line. At the creek, there's a one-lane bridge, a little whitewater, stones exactly the right size for braining — which is what we come within inches of before we move The Toad downstream, well away from his brother. The sun shines for, give or take, the first time all weekend. Both boys are throwing rocks now, laughing and hollering, and the sound of those stones in the creek, the sound of the creek and these boys — I close my eyes and try to hang on to all of it. Nobody's hurt yet. Everybody's happy. I'd reach out for my wife's hand, but she's making sure whichever child she's in charge of stays on dry land. Maybe later tonight, then. Maybe in those first few empty moments after kid bedtime. For now, it's plenty excellent to be in both places, both lives, at once. *O*s

Elk Creek Valley Loop

• ALLEGHANY COUNTY •

An 18-mile driving loop through western Alleghany County will take you past scenic vistas and historical landmarks. You'll wind along back roads and up on ridges, driving alongside and across Elk Creek. For more information, visit sparta-nc.com/maps.php.

IN A SEAPLANE ON THE CHOWAN RIVER

You don't have to leave the ground to watch imagination take flight.

We're winging down U.S. Highway 158 very early on a Sunday, in the flatlands of northeastern North Carolina. I'm undercaffeinated. The Toad is not. The two of us are in search of the Chowan River — in particular, of the Chowan River Rats, North Carolina's only true seaplane operation. I have sent the River Rats an email that says: *My son. He's obsessed with seaplanes. Is there any possibility ...?* And the River Rats have come through with, well, flying colors: *Sure. No problem at all.*

(We are not, though, to fly. My wife has veto power in

matters of earth vs. sky. This is a sit-in-the-cockpit-only type of deal.)

For months, The Toad has wanted to discuss seaplanes. Daily. Hourly. He has questions upon questions: How far can they fly? Who gets to drive them? Can we build a real one out of paper? Are they very, very loud? Once, at dinner, we somehow decided that green paint could never be on seaplanes — not as cargo, not as decoration. This stuck, became a rule, became the foil for epic, tangled stories — my favorite involves Goldilocks and the Three Bears, who have reconciled and are traveling as a family, having their seaplane vacation upended because Goldilocks is wearing green fingernail polish.

The Chowan, when we do find it, is wide and serene, possessed of great beauty. Not too many miles from here, it goes tidal, empties into Albemarle Sound. It's quiet. There are birds. I want, basically, to quit my life, to move into the round, red-roofed waterfront house belonging to the River Rats — whose seaplane, of course, is striped green. "Daddy!" says The Toad, eyes bright. Up is down, wrong is right, lions are lying down with lambs. Green paint. He just points. He doesn't even say it.

"Well," I tell him, "we'll have to ask Mr. Joyner about that."

Mr. Joyner is Henry Joyner, River Rat One of two (the other is his son; those are their call signs). He's 60ish, and dressed like he owns a seaplane: sandals, ripstop shorts, neon yellow T-shirt, orange windbreaker. I get the sense that should we require a low-key yet swashbuckling rescue, Joyner would be our man. He's very patient. He shakes The Toad's hand. He loads us onto the plane, a gorgeous two-seat 1946 Piper Super Cruiser that smells deeply familiar, a gas-oil memory of my father mowing the lawn. The seats are leather. The inside's green, too. The Toad is sufficiently thrilled, if a little overwhelmed. Pretty soon, he wants off. He wants to go back to the car to get his toy seaplane. Just like that, he's done.

Henry Joyner squints out at the far bank, smiles. "You drove three hours," he says, "for him to be on there 10 minutes?"

"Tell me about seaplanes," I say, ducking his question. The Toad floats his toy in the shadow of the real thing. Joyner says, "I like that you can land anywhere. You're not bound to some slab of concrete." He tells me the whole plane's probably been rebuilt 10 times. There's something about re-skinning the wings that I don't totally understand, but I touch the plane, as though that will help. He says that, when flying, you're supposed to stay low enough "to where if the engine quits, you can land with minimal damage to life and property." I confess: I start to suspect he might also be talking about parenthood. Or just being on the planet in the first place. I'm convinced of this when he says that the most difficult landing is on calm, glassy water: It's almost impossible to tell where the surface is. You have to fly closely over something on land — a "last visual reference point" — and then set your descent, trusting and hoping that the plane finds the water. He doesn't belabor these points. He just lets them lie. And when The Toad asks if he can get on a second time, Henry Joyner says, "Sure."

This time around, the child is comfortable, babbling, excited. We're on his terms. He steers, he checks the gauges. We refuel, apparently in midair. He tells me I should buckle my seat belt, tells me he'll be a pilot when he's 5. The doors are open. There's a breeze off the river. We're bobbing on the surface. Fifteen minutes. Twenty. We're River Rats. I don't want to leave. A good part of me wants to risk my marriage, ask if we can fly. It's not just The Toad who thinks so: Being on a seaplane is really, really cool.

But Joyner's noontime client arrives. The plane is not, as it turns out, very loud. They practice takeoffs and landings, touching down right in front of us on the Chowan, then lifting off again. It's delicate and Hollywood all at the same time. The third or fourth time they do this, The Toad realizes he forgot to ask about the green paint. "I guess it's a mystery," he says. No lie. I tell him, "I guess it is," and we watch the plane fly downriver until it's out of sight, until it's hard to say for sure if it was ever even there. *Os*

OBX Biplanes

• MANTEO •

For a new perspective, take a tour of the Outer Banks by air in an open-cockpit biplane. See lighthouses, schools of fish, pods of dolphins, and more when you cruise over the ocean with a pilot as your guide. For more information, call (252) 216-7777, or visit obxbiplanes.com.

LIKE RIDING A BIKE

Things don't always go exactly the way you planned — and that's half the fun.

Practice makes
perfect. Next stop
for Drew and The
Toad: the Little Sugar
Creek Greenway in
Charlotte.

The night in question: one of those short-sleeves-to-sweatshirts Piedmont evenings, a star or two

winking on, the sun dropping through the western end of the neighborhood. Those of us playing at being adults are scattered in chairs at the bottom of the backyard hill. Kids are everywhere: in the playroom, watching movies. In the kitchen, sneaking cake. In a tree house, bashing each other with toy swords. Occasionally somebody asks the kids to sword-fight a bit more gently. Then the wine comes around again.

From the top of the hill, The Toad hollers down, asks me something — and then here he comes. On somebody else's balance bike — the pedal-less, pre-bicycle kind. He's been asking for a balance bike for weeks. Months. We've told him no. The bike shop guy suggested against it. Said if we could get him on his own pedal bike, that'd be better. I shaved our backyard to putting-green height, stripped the training wheels off The Toad's Huffy — at his request — and spent several afternoons doing the dad-holds-the-seat-and-runs thing, as seen on whatever joint-pain ask-your-doctor TV commercial you care to imagine. Each afternoon ended in abject parental failure. "Pedal!" you yelled, if you were me. "I am pedaling!" you yelled, if you were The Toad, lying on the ground, underneath your bike.

But where were we? Crystalline light. Neighborhood party. The Toad emerging from the dusk, balanced perfectly, barefoot, helmetless, steering right through conversations about mortgages and magnet schools. There are no brakes on a balance bike. He comes to rest against the gas grill. The gas grill is not on. No toads are harmed in the making of this scene. He's not smiling. He's not triumphant. You want to know what he is? Unsurprised.

He's not surprised 10 minutes later when he does it on a bike with pedals, either. Nor that weekend, when he's looping figure eights around an empty outdoor basketball court.

THE DEAL HAS BEEN THIS: AS SOON AS HE LEARNS TO ride, I'll get a bicycle, too, so I can ride with him. I decide I'll save a little money by ordering it online. The box arrives. It is about the size of an adult bike, which is fortunate, because the boys can play in the box for the 14 hours it takes to put the bike together. "Take tools your first time out," my mother says, laughing at me on the phone. When the handlebars fall off in my hand later that evening in the park, I call her back to tell her she was right.

We need a destination. A maiden voyage. We practice

a little at home, then decide to head for Charlotte, for the Little Sugar Creek Greenway. A day trip. To celebrate. Somewhere safe, somewhere flat, somewhere with no cars. Perhaps a picnic. I ask The Toad what he'd like to take, and he says pickles, tomatoes, potato chips, chocolate syrup, and sandwiches. I pack most of that.

That space between what you imagine a thing might be and what it is: These days, I live almost exclusively right there. In my head, I have us biking for miles, in and out of reforested streambed, emerging to look at the glittering skyline. Tall buildings! Progress! I'll gloss the history of urban green space. We'll chat architecture.

In reality, we stop every 70 feet. No lie. And not because The Toad can't ride. He's fine. He just — how to put this? — he has the attention span of a 4-year-old. We stop to look at the creek. We stop to look at rocks in the creek. We stop to climb on things. All things. Stairs. Hills. Landscaping. Art. And who's nearly killed? Me. One of the few times we're both up and pedaling, I make an attempt to snap a few pictures with one hand and steer with the other. I get a pretty immediate sense of what it would be like to land in Little Sugar Creek.

We eat our lunch, we play in Freedom Park, we spend almost as much time in Charlotte as it takes to get there. The greenway is immaculate, the day perfect and warm, domed with a high blue sky. If The Toad were older, we'd bail on the whole picnic thing, spend all day, bike one end to the other, eat at any one of the restaurants along the way. Maybe places like this are a little sanitized — idealized versions of what it means to live in any one spot — but that's the version I want for now, anyway. The Toad believes in Santa and magic and interstellar travel. Why not this, too? He points out a skyscraper, asks if the little girl from Charlotte we met at the beach last year lives there. I tell him it's for sure either that one or the next one over.

We pass some unmarked milestone down there, of course — because there's my kid, riding a bike, and there's me, following him. We're both in helmets, to save us from ourselves. The greenway stretches out in front of us. We could go forever. Or we could stop, again and again and again, to look at bugs, to look at sticks, to look at bugs on sticks. I brought him down to see the city. He'll have little of that. He wants to show me the world. **Os**

Little Sugar Creek Greenway

• CHARLOTTE •

In the middle of Charlotte's urban jungle, you'll find Little Sugar Creek Greenway, which offers miles of paved trails along a restored stream. Whether you're socializing, exercising, or just seeking a quiet moment in nature, this greenway has you covered. For more information, visit charmeck.org.

A SUPER SLIDE & EVERYTHING FRIED

A lesson on living in the moment and making it count, courtesy of the State Fair.

First one down the Super Slide gets a deep-fried treat. Bonus points for putting your hands in the air.

The Super Slide. For a full calendar year, he's talked about the Super Slide. That was his favorite. Not the head-size snow cone you bought him for four bucks. Not the helicopters and construction machinery parked on an island out in the lake. Not the racing pigs you did not see, but ended up explaining for weeks on end, often at bedtime. How and why a racing pig works its way into nighttime prayers and ablutions:

This is the kind of thing you've learned not to question.

Also good, but not *as* good: the frozen lemonade that made his little brother actually groan with pleasure. The funnel cake. The deep-fried barbecue, the deep-fried mac and cheese, the Krispy Kreme burger. The dragon ride that lumbered up into the air and down again. The wash and spin of all the signs, the loudspeakers, the barkers. The spendy bicycle taxi you rode from the parking lot. But was any of that the Super Slide? It was not. Daddy. Daddy. Over and over again. Daddy, do you remember the Super Slide?

RIGHT AWAY — AS IN, FIRST FOOT OUT OF THE CAR — YOU step in gum. It is not a crisp fall day. It is the other kind of Carolina October, the kind that isn't yet ready to give up summer. From the back seat, though, The Toad, fresh off a fairly fierce car ride, says, "I love this day." Write that down, OK? Get the gum off your shoe and find a pen. You think you'll remember these things. You always think that. Then you forget. He'll have something to say about the evening sky. His first peanut brittle. The banjo player in the bluegrass band, who says, just as you walk past, "Well, y'all, this is our final set at the State Fair."

The toddler's in a backpack, but the The Toad is loose, so here's what happens: Somebody official gets you to put a sticker with your phone number and address inside his shirt, in case he gets separated from you. In case he gets lost. He wants to know what lost means, how a thing like that might happen. He's a cautious boy. Lots of questions. You tell him not to worry, that nobody's getting lost, that everything's going to be fine. "Then why do I need a sticker?" he wants to know. Distract him with livestock. With plastic swords. With a flashlight given away by a disaster insurance company.

Work your way past the clowns on stilts, the acrobats hanging from streamers, the fire-safety demonstration. Feed the boys. Feed them again. Find the kiddie rides. Somebody who's leaving, with two red-faced children of his own in tow, hands you a ream of sweaty tickets. "Here," he says. "Just take these." It does not quite feel like a gift, even if it is a kindness.

The kiddie coaster. The aforementioned dragons. The Ferris wheel, which does not seem kid-size at all, where you try very hard to conceal from the big one your serious fear of heights (the little one's back on the ground with his mom). And then? The Super Slide. Which is not that super, in your estimation. It is 15 minutes of waiting in line, of cajoling and threatening and begging the child to behave, to wait, to use good manners, even though he is hot and tired and super-sugared and has never actually waited in line before and thus has no idea what the hell is going on. The slide itself: maybe 70 feet. You sit bobsled-style on a burlap bag. A couple of humps. Not so steep. You land on a gym mat. And that's the whole thing.

He *loves* it. It is exactly his speed. He wants to do it again. And again. Somehow, it's evening now. The sky purples, the breeze freshens. All around you, the same dance: One more, but then we have to go. It's hard to imagine that all these booths and games and people will pack up and ride away. It's hard to understand that you've been here however many hours. Maybe time doesn't really operate at the fair. Finally, you take them home. Because the little one's asleep in his pack. Because somewhere it's an actual o'clock. Because you're out of tickets. Because you're tired. Because one of these times down the slide has to be the last.

And for one year, you'll be sorry. You'll remember driving home into the rising moon, wishing, already, that you'd let him ride one more time. The Super Slide. He doesn't understand that the State Fair comes only once a year. That, like a racing pig, it's an article of faith. When it comes back, you'll tell him each time he asks, we'll go. You'll promise: Yes, we can ride the Super Slide. Yes, as many times as you like. Yes, you'll tell him, all year, as much as possible. And this year, you'll tell him, your brother can ride, too. *Os*

NC State Fair

· RALEIGH ·

A quintessential North Carolina experience. For two weeks each October, the State Fair celebrates our state and its agricultural heritage, and offers a healthy dose of indulgence — deep-fried Oreos, funnel cakes, and turkey legs, anyone? — plus entertainment, rides, and, yes, the Super Slide. For more information, call (919) 733-2145 or visit ncstatefair.org.

SEARCHING FOR PIRATES ON THE CRYSTAL COAST

An adventure begins long before you reach your destination. Make time for fun along the way.

When it comes to searching for pirates, one needs a keen eye and an adventurous spirit. The Toad has both, plus binoculars.

We weren't even going to go
on a honeymoon. We'd made
the catastrophic decision to
do the whole wedding

ourselves — we even grew white petunias in little pots for
the giveaway centerpieces. We were so tired that when it
came my turn to take the microphone, I forgot to thank
anybody. I forgot to tell people to take the petunias. All
I said was that if it did storm, which it was trying to do,
then the caterers would leave and we'd all be on our own
to tend bar. We were so tired that, later, we actually fell
asleep in the tub.

But we got the sense that we should do *something*.
That Monday, we made a series of half-comatose phone
calls until somebody took pity on us and said yes, we
could come to the beach in a last-minute, midweek,
high-season way. That somebody was the Atlantis Lodge
in Pine Knoll Shores. I remember a high school kid —
Jared? — who would set your umbrella in the sand for
you, which seemed quite the luxury. I remember high
school girls vying for Jared's attention. I remember
that the whole place was kitted out in a kind of piece-
meal mod groove, as if Peter Sellers had quit those
pharmaceutically-fueled 1960s dinner-party comedies,
stolen half the set decorations, and reinvented himself as

an oceanfront hotelier on the Crystal Coast. I remember little else; the kids have, for me, anyway, wiped a lot of the pre-kids days pretty clean.

At least, though, when The Toad announces that he'd like to see pirates — for real life, as he says — I know exactly where to take him. One night, just the two of us. The Toad is, shall we say, a touch cranked up. He's eaten the mints off the bedside table. He's got his binoculars at the ready. He is also wearing two different days-of-the-week socks — Sunday on his left foot, Tuesday on his right — and jumping on the bed.

Forgive me, good people of the Atlantis: I let him. In two days I'll be 40 years old, which for so long seemed to be a construct rather than an actual thing. I stand out on the wooden balcony and stare at the glittering, open ocean, and think, *We thought we were tired?* I think, *I miss you. This place is exactly the same. It's wonderful. It's impossibly strange to be here without you.* I think other things, too, but The Toad's blue bear, Azulito, is now scream-singing "Jingle Bells," months out of season, in a grating, ventriloquized falsetto, which leaves little room for much else.

BEAUFORT, JUST UP THE ROAD AND OVER THE BRIDGE, is both the former home of Blackbeard and the third-oldest city in North Carolina. Captain Barrel tells us this the next morning as we chart a course on the not-at-all high seas. His name is actually Captain Barrow, of Island Ferry Adventures, but The Toad mishears because he's begging me to ask Captain Barrel if he'll let him drive. Captain Barrel is no fool; this is not his first — well, whatever the seafaring equivalent of a rodeo is. He quits his history lesson midstream and produces a wooden stool, picks up The Toad, tells him to sit on his knees, and there's my son spinning the wheel back and forth, squinting, grinning, wind in his hair. Captain Toad. I take 400 pictures. Then I get smart and quit, and just watch.

Though there are wild horses and trails through a spectacular maritime forest out on Carrot Island — where Captain Barrel drops us off — there seems to be no buried treasure. Nor pirates. This is a source of such great disappointment that The Toad cares basically not at all about the flock of blue herons that fly by at chest height right in front of us on the north beach. "Do you have sad?" I ask him, because 24 hours without adult conversation leaves me lost in kidspeak. "No," he says, kicking the sand. "I have boring." I tell him that we probably ought to start walking back, because if the tide comes in, we're going to be stranded out on this shoal. "Awesome!" he says, perking right back up.

And we do find pirates back onshore, in the North Carolina Maritime Museum, so all is well. We purchase a Blackbeard T-shirt, and The Toad wears that thing out of the gift shop like it's a new pair of shoes from the Stride-Rite at the mall. Plus this — I have to say this: The first night, the only night, bedded down together for the first time since he was an infant, The Toad says, "Daddy. Do not let me get eated, and do not let me get dead. And do not let me catch on fire."

"OK," I say. "I will not."

"And if any of those things happen to you," he says, "I will stop them from happening, and you will be all set."

"Thank you," I say.

He says, "You have to protect me."

"That's my job," I say.

"It is also your job to work with your computer, and work with utensils, and play with me," he says.

"That's right," I say, rolling over, grabbing a pad, writing all that down. I want to be able to tell his mom. I want to remember. I want to mark an X on the map. *Os*

Island Ferry Adventures

· BEAUFORT ·

For $10, Island Ferry Adventures in Beaufort will transport you to the nearby barrier islands to explore for an hour or the whole day. If your destination is Carrot Island, you can explore salt marshes, look for sand dollars, or just relax on the beach. For more information, call (252) 728-4129, or visit islandferryadventures.com.

AND TO ALL A GOOD NIGHT

*On family ties, blue Christmas lights,
and waiting for Santa Claus.*

The idea of Santa can be unnerving when you're little; it helps if he makes a quiet entrance.

DEAR SANTA,
PLEASE DON'T RING YOUR SLEIGH BELLS.
LOVE,
ME

The Christmas The Toad was 3½ years old, we went all in on Santa. Over the course of that year, the child had become a person who could carry on something resembling a conversation, so the time seemed right. Big dude in a red suit, we told him. Flying reindeer. Serious operation based out of the North Pole.

We sent a letter to this "Santa." We went to see him at the mall. We explained all about how Santa would rooftop himself at some point between bedtime on Christmas Eve and whenever we woke up on Christmas morning. We made fairly assiduous efforts to be nice, rather than naughty. All December long, we read *The Night Before Christmas*.

On the actual night before Christmas, I took The Toad out to the front porch to listen for sleigh bells. Then we went upstairs for a long winter's nap. Important, I guess, to note that The Toad was and is a child who wishes very much to know precisely what is coming next. Who fears, sometimes acutely, things like thunderstorms and substitute teachers and surprise in general and — I got all the way to his bedroom door before I realized he'd started crying. "Sweetheart," I asked him, "what's wrong?"

He did not want to hear sleigh bells in the night. This he told me between sobs. Here's what I'd done: I'd spent a month telling my kid, the kid who reacts to change the way most folks react to electric shock, that a magic, fur-clad stranger was going to land on his roof in a hail of jingling bells and reindeer hooves, enter his house through the chimney, eat his cookies and drink his milk, drop a few things off, and then skulk back out again. I climbed in his bed. I held him. I told him I was sorry. Fortunately, he did not ask me what I was sorry for.

"Daddy," he said, once he got calm. "Here's what I want you to do. Write a note that says, 'Dear Santa, Please don't ring your sleigh bells. Love, Me.'" Then he told me he wanted me to put the note "backwards" in the window, by which he meant: letters facing out. That, I told him, we could do. And I did. I made the sign and hung it up and kissed him goodnight, and he asked me for one more favor: "Stand outside and wait for Santa," he said. "Tell him to make sure to look in my window. Tell him to read the note." I said I would. And before I could tell him I loved him, The Toad said, "I love you, too."

A HISTORY OF SCOTS IN NORTH CAROLINA THAT WENDS its way Toadward would trace certain members of Clan Mackay — a clan (like all clans, surely) known for heroism and bravery — down out of the Highlands of Scotland and across the ocean and into the Upper Cape Fear River Basin. Let's call that 1750ish. At some point, Mackay becomes McKay. At some later point, my grandfather Walter McKay marries my grandmother Jane. At some point later still, they decide to hang blue lights — and blue lights only — on the house at Christmas, to celebrate their Scottish heritage.

It was in the glow of those lights — the actual lights from my grandmother's front porch, large-bulbed lights I drove hours to claim when we sold her house, lights I now hang each Christmas on my own house — that I waited for St. Nick. Maybe I snuck back inside to find a cup of wassail. Maybe I listened in on the monitor to see if all was well upstairs. But The Toad, fierce descendant of Clan Mackay, would certainly ask me the next morning, and I did not want to lie. Yes, I needed to be able to say. Yes, I sat out there in the blue, just like you asked.

I'LL STAND OUTSIDE ON CHRISTMAS EVE, EVEN IF JUST for a few minutes, for the rest of my life. It's not so hard to know when a tradition is born. I'll stand out there in the blue lights — I will baby those lights back to life each year, no matter what it takes — and I'll wait.

I'll wait because he asked me if I would. I'll wait years after he no longer needs such a thing. I'll wait because I'm a person who all but clings to the quieter moments of holidays: I'm a big fan of the day before. I like the getting ready. The holding still. The waiting, under your grandmother's blue lights, for something impossible.

I'll stand out there in a Carolina evening that's just cold enough, maybe, to offer the possibility of snow. I'll look to the east, toward the lands of The Toad's transplanted Scottish ancestry. I'll watch the sky for Santa. "Read the note," I'll be ready to say. "We left you a note. If you wouldn't mind, please land quietly." **Os**

Santa on the Chimney

• CHIMNEY ROCK STATE PARK •

In order to successfully climb down millions of chimneys on Christmas Eve, Santa knows that practice makes perfect. Catch up with the man in red on two "training days" in December, when he heads to Hickory Nut Gorge, scales the 315-foot Chimney Rock, and rappels back down — assisted by his elves, of course. Meet Mr. and Mrs. Claus and enjoy live holiday music, hot cocoa, and more. For more information, visit chimneyrockpark.com.

Big feet, little feet: Drew and The Toad put their camping skills, and tent, to the test — in their backyard.

CAMPING
IN YOUR OWN
BACKYARD

Life's simplest pleasures are always close to home.

The original plan was to rent a tent from Campus Rec (I work at a university; said university has recreational facilities and equipment, both). We were never going to rent sleeping bags, though. The rental of coed sleeping bags seems a dubious prospect, even when considered in the very best light. Plus, we reasoned, the kids would love having their own sleeping bags. We'd use them for movie nights. Room-to-room sleepovers when the little one gets less little. But then I blew up half a stick of butter inside the microwave. We were making waffles. From scratch. The recipe wanted melted butter. In the aftermath of that incident, my whole belief system seemed to waver a little. If the inside of the microwave can look like *this*, I thought, who could say what else might befall us? We might *need* a tent someday.

So we bought a tent, too.

And let's save ourselves the trouble of the tent-poles-and-rain-fly montage, some jolly song playing in the background while I nearly put my eye out trying to make a four-person dome from something that comes in a sack the size of two lunchboxes. Let's slide past the moment when I'm still holding way too many stakes and haven't yet discovered that there are more directions on the back of the directions. Let's move directly to The Toad tunneling headfirst into his sleeping bag, yelling out, "Where am I? Where am I?" Or to The Wee bedding down in his own bag, holding an open children's umbrella in one hand, and in the other, a bear named Puppy who speaks in meows. Probably we'll just use whatever college fund remains, when the time comes, for therapy for that bear.

THE BULK OF THIS EXERCISE — THE KIDS-ON-PURPOSE exercise — has been, for me, about learning to love the noise. My wife achieves this brand of Zen a little more readily than I do. Which was the look she kept giving me from the other side of the tent: Breathe. Take it in. So I did. I lay down on the ground, our ground, our own however-many square feet of North Carolina, and listened to the noise of our backyard. The boys, sure. But also: trains. From this yard, this little Greensboro hill, there are almost always trains. And birds, signaling the season. And dogs all up and down the street. Traffic out on the bigger road that's a block behind the church. The bell tower in that church. Wind, high up in the huge sweet gums next door.

(Later, when it got dark, The Wee turned on his flashlight, held the business end of the thing against his open eye, and said, "Eyes. Eyes." I'm noting that here just to keep from getting too sentimental. Too sweet-gummed.)

I don't know what patch of land I know better than

this fraction of an acre. The hydrangeas and black-eyed Susans and cornflowers. The poison ivy I poison a couple of times a year. The daffodils we planted; the ones that were already here. The green-blooming gladiolas that I love so much. The Kousa dogwood. The volunteer cherry tomatoes. Remember, kids, when Daddy used to garden? No, you do not. And although the neighbors may resent you, the crabgrass does not, nor the dollarweed, if that is indeed what's replaced the fescue. What should we do about the hole over there, in front of the cherry trees, where the basement sump drains? You guys just want to keep riding your bikes through it? Good enough. And speaking of bikes: There are bikes, a plastic police car, a formerly battery-powered ATV, most of a basketball goal, the remains of a baseball tee, some kind of over-size nylon Frisbee — hey, please stop throwing mulch in the yard. Watch out for that flower bed. Careful of the azaleas. Please, just —

I hadn't been in a tent in 20 years. Not since Boy Scouts. I was once on a campout so rainy that the tent next to ours cut loose from its moorings, and the kids inside floated by, singing "Yellow Submarine." But there was none of that on this backyard night. We didn't even sleep out there. I have to tell the truth. We just wanted them to know what a tent was. The Wee would never have gone to sleep, and, by the looks of things, The Toad might not have crashed until sunrise. We did, though, let them stay up well past their bedtimes, and we lay on either edge of the tent while the boys went bonkers between us, laughing and bashing each other with their flashlights and making plans to fly us to the moon.

I loved it, OK? I loved being in that small square. I

loved all of us in there. At one point, The Toad pulled on his brother's leg, hard, and The Wee kicked him in the head. The Toad complained. You deserved that, I told him, but then apologized, pulled him to me, and then somehow each of us grown-ups ended up with one boy in a grown-up sleeping bag. That didn't last for more than about 10 minutes, but nothing ever does these days. I had The Toad. My wife had The Wee. Breathe it in, she was telling me. I am, I was telling her. I am. *Os*

Carolina Hemlocks Recreation Area

• BURNSVILLE •

For an overnight adventure a bit farther from home, check out Carolina Hemlocks Recreation Area and Campground in the Pisgah National Forest, an hour outside of Asheville. One of the most popular and family-friendly camping spots in the state, it sits alongside the South Toe River, offering a great place to explore, swim, fish, and tube. For more information, call (828) 675-5509, or visit cfaia.org.

MARS, BY WAY OF CAROLINA

When you've staked out your own little corner of the night sky, the names of the stars don't matter as much as the time you spend looking up.

Drew conducts an informal lesson in astronomy, tailored to the interests of The Toad and The Wee.

We're a bit of a show. Maybe more than a bit. Neither kid will sit in the cart anymore, and now, free-ranging through the grocery, they're tracing some unnamed land between circus and calamity. The Wee, when he's not seeking out breakable items, is shrieking, "Yike! Yike! Dragons!" He's 2. He hands his yikes out one at a time.

The Toad, for his part, is going on at extraordinary length about Mars. He's in kindergarten now, knows a great many things. Mars is the only planet where aliens live. There are good aliens and bad aliens. Or maybe there are only good aliens? He checks to see if I know. I do not know. The Wee arrives with a glass jar of something, throws it in the cart. It does not break. "Mars is as far away as from my room to Alaska," The Toad says.

We rocket around an endcap featuring a sugared cereal that the kids heretofore had not known existed. "Please," they say. "Please!" "No," I tell them. And that's our call-and-response for an aisle or two, until they start sword-fighting with a pair of Slim Jims. I get down on my knees, skip right through threats to bribery: If they can have good manners the rest of the way, then we can purchase, and even consume, hot chocolate.

"But then can we find a dark place to look for Mars?" The Toad asks, holding steady. For a few weeks — since the Mars thing cropped up — we've been talking about sky-watching. "Will you take me to a dark place? Do you know any?"

Kid, I want to say, *parenting can get you to some pretty dark places.* Instead, I tell him that I know a great spot. I stand up, and a stranger says to me, "Sir, you must be exhausted." He's youngish, college-age, at a place in his life where he's still sleeping in. The Wee's been up since 6 a.m., when he appeared like a ghost in our room, announcing: "I wake up." I laugh and tell the stranger it's not so bad. What I don't tell him, because I don't want to scare him, is that things are going pretty well. As trips to the grocery go, this one's been easy. No yelling, no crying, no blood or bone. Only dragons and aliens. And Mars.

WHERE DO YOU TAKE A KID TO SHOW HIM THE NIGHT sky? The backyard will do fine; children don't understand light pollution, wouldn't know to miss the Milky Way. I have memories, though, of my father standing in my grandmother's pitch-black yard, pointing out constellations by flashlight beam. If there are six ways I think of him, then that's one, him showing me Orion's Belt where all I saw were stars. "Do you see it?" he asked me. I lied until I did.

Their grandmother's yard, then. My mother-in-law's. She lives up the side of a mountain just outside of Asheville, has a driveway that's plenty dark and a clearing that looks south into a winter sky more than full enough to do the job. Not that I don't show The Toad the sky before we get there, but we play it up: *The stars are the best at your Abi's house. Wait till we see the stars at Abi's. Just you wait.*

There is a hitch: Mars is up after midnight this winter, and we flirt with the wee hours enough as it is. Still, each night of our visit, we make hot chocolate — The Toad forgets nothing — and bundle the kids against the cold and the dark, and we go out there. The driveway is so steep as to make using it an adventure, but that lends itself perfectly to lying on your back and looking at the sky. I have no flashlight and the kids are dribbling hot chocolate everywhere and The Wee's mug at some point goes rolling off down the hill, but they're into it. Both of them. "Which one is Mars?" The Toad wants to know. "It's not up there," I tell him. "But it's in outer space," he says. "Yes," I say. "So is that one Mars?" he asks — and I tell him yes. The Wee gets ahold of this rhythm and asks again and again, seemingly about every star. "Yes," I say. "That one, too. They're all Mars."

This makes them laugh, and that makes me cry, because I get sentimental around this time of year, and because the sound of these two boys laughing — not slamming doors or kicking each other or stomping, wronged and furious, up the stairs — is all the New Year's resolution I ever hope to need. How can I get them to make that sound again?

For now, the answer's right in front of us: Let's just keep playing this game. Let's lie on our backs on the frigid driveway and look up. Let's misname each and every star in the Carolina sky. *Os*

Morehead Planetarium

• CHAPEL HILL •

You won't have to worry about light pollution, cloudy nights, or keeping the little ones up too late when you visit the Morehead Planetarium. One of its longest-running shows, "Carolina Skies," focuses on the stars, planets, and constellations that can be seen above our state. For more information, call (919) 918-1155, or visit moreheadplanetarium.org.

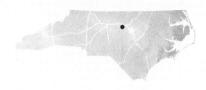

TO FIND A
FIREWORK

You might find louder, more impressive pyrotechnics south of the border, but you won't find the Lottaburger.

The noise-averse
Toad finds solace
in sparklers,
those tiny, silent
fireworks you can
hold in your hands.

We are certainly not driving south on Interstate 85 to cross the border to buy Roman candles — which are legal in *that* Carolina, but outlawed in ours. Here, you can buy sparklers, and not much else. There, you can probably buy howitzers. But no matter: That's not what we're up to. We're just driving 125 miles to grab a quick lunch, looking for a restaurant in Kings Mountain called Blackwood's Drive-In. Blackwood's is the self-professed Home of the Lottaburger. I don't know what that is, but as a general rule, the boys like burgers. I like burgers. Everybody likes a two-hour drive with small children. The fact that Kings Mountain is within eight miles of the border has nothing to do with anything. At all.

Earlier that week, discussing pyrotechnics with my wife, I said, "North Carolina doesn't want you to have the fun kind."

"That," she said, "or South Carolinians don't mind getting their fingers blown off."

GREENSBORO IS THE FIREWORKINGEST PLACE I'VE EVER lived. Fireworks are our searchlights. We fire off professional (and therefore permissible) displays from concert venues, car dealerships, malls, waterparks, and higher-end fifth-grade graduations. We have Fourth of July shows. We have makeup dates for the rained-out Fourth of July shows. The baseball team, delightfully overeager, celebrates Friday nights, Saturday nights, home runs, and the national anthem — with fireworks. Even the universities get in on the action. It is no exaggeration to say that on any given summer evening, you might not have to try terribly hard to find big-boy, full-bore fireworks around here — which is among the city's finest features.

We bought our house, in fact, partly for its proximity to the stadium. I can watch the ballpark fireworks from my front porch. But we bought the house before we had kids. Before we had our older son, who's turned out not to be a big fan of big noise. He is anti-thunderstorm. Anti-firework. His little brother, though? Here is the difference between them: When I break out the coffee grinder in the mornings, The Toad flees the room, hands over his ears. The Wee claps and dances, asks for more.

I'm sorry, The Toad! Sorry for your firework of a brother, for the house with its hundred-year-old windows rattling in their casings after the game, for living on a Piedmont plain that offers up few truly severe summer storms, but all manner of crash and bang. Your grandfather once sat me down in front of a screen door at the height of a massive thunderstorm, held me tight in his lap while wind blew rain through the metal screen — a smell and taste I can recall right now — and converted me to loud. Forever. Fireworks included. Might we find some way to make a convert out of you?

Your brother, of course, will need no shock therapy. He loves loud. Or youd, as he's been saying. He'll point at the drill, at the vacuum, up at the sky, and yell YOUD! YOUD! Meanwhile, you, if you're awake, huddle elsewhere, presumably with the guardian ghost-angel of our first dog, who also hated all things youd.

It is a delicate dance around here, the youd versus the not-youd.

I'M NOT EVEN CERTAIN, AT FIRST, THAT I'LL BE ABLE TO stand up inside Blackwood's: The white-brick building is that small. (We didn't hazard the actual drive-in part of the deal; toddlers do not eat in-car.) But the Lottaburger is a thing of a certain kind of beauty: two patties, side by side, on a seeded hoagie bun. Two slabs of tomato. Half a cup of creamy slaw. Pickles. It is delicious. It is a catastrophe. I am right away glad for having brought the kids a change of clothes.

I love this place with a sparkling fierceness, is what I'm trying to say.

Also, there are onion rings. Fried corn nuggets. Our waitress, who is wearing a Wonder Woman T-shirt, tells the boys that she in fact *is* Wonder Woman — and they are delighted to believe this. We try hard to spend $20 and don't even come close. We had to wait to get a table at 3 in the afternoon. There are paper plates and Styrofoam cups. Ice cream and milkshakes. I love this place with a sparkling fierceness, is what I'm trying to say. It is a dive, in the holiest sense of that word.

We eat and go home. We do not drive any farther south. Which means, of course, that the fireworks we light that night — it is the season, after all — are the kind you can buy from any number of pop-up tents at North Carolina gas stations this time of year. They are plain. Mainly safe. And fairly quiet, I assure The Toad. There's still plenty of magic to it, though, as we light the fuse, cover our ears, and watch the sky. The ground, I mean. Nothing that leaves the ground is legal here. Not for civilians, anyway. I pull both boys close — the one who's scared, the one who's not — and, with our bellies full, we watch the ground. *Os*

Blackwood's Drive-In

· KINGS MOUNTAIN ·

You'd be hard-pressed to find a more classic American spot than Blackwood's, which has been serving old-fashioned flat-top grill fare, crinkle fries, and milkshakes for more than 30 years. For the most authentic experience, order the Lottaburger with a Cherry Lemon Sun Drop. For more information, call (704) 730-8899.

A DAY AT THE ZOO

Alligators to zebras and even the gift shop:
Everything's a wonder at the
North Carolina Zoo in Asheboro.

Say hello to a harbor seal at the North Carolina Zoo's Rocky Coast exhibit.

"Rule number three," says The Toad. "Never, ever get close to biting animals." He's a tour guide, has snapped into the role with startling efficiency. We've been at the zoo for maybe five minutes. No one has any idea what the other two rules are. "Look," he tells his little brother, taking him by the hand, walking him over to one wall. "We can learn about peregrine falcons right here."

We hang back, my wife and I. This is the season of hanging back. Of letting the kids, finally able to do a handful of things for themselves, do things for themselves. We have no hope of seeing the whole North Carolina Zoo anyway. The Toad is 5½; his brother, The Wee, is nearly 3. Their attention spans will survive neither the morning nor the emergence, a few enclosures over from the peregrine falcon's, of the Arctic fox. "THAT IS SO AWESOME," The Toad says. The fox looks like a cross between a dog and a cat in sheep's clothing. "I want to be an Arctic fox!" he says. "I want to have creature powers!" I tell him he can. This idea holds the lion's share of his attention until we see actual lions. Though that isn't true: We see many animals, but no lions. The Arctic fox holds him until we see a soda machine. Then he loses his mind. Then we lose our minds, and buy him a soda.

THE WATANI GRASSLANDS MAY BE THE SHOWSTOPPER here, a breathtaking, wide-open savanna that immediately puts aside most concerns one might have about the ethics of zoos. The whole of the NC Zoo does, really, and it should: Constructed at a time when the country was rethinking zoos, it was the first to radically reimagine ideas of habitat and captivity, seeking to provide animals with space to be, well, animals. "What's that called?" The Wee asks, pointing at an oryx, which is a kind of antelope.

"It's an oryx," I tell him. "It's a kind of antelope."

"Oh," he says. Much of the day goes this way: After the initial thrills of the harbor seals and the sleeping polar bear, and the children's near-complete delight at just riding the tram between North America and Africa, we fall mainly into pointing and naming. The Toad is interested in the elephants, but more interested in the coin-operated binoculars. The Wee is interested in the oryx, but more interested in handfuls of rocks. The zoo has prepared for difficulties such as these: Placed behind where my wife and I would like to stand and watch actual rhinoceroses moving across an actual plain, there are child-size ostrich eggs in which children might play while their parents consider the wonder of the natural world. This works fine until someone bonks his head on something. Then there are tears. These we mollify — we're weak, OK? — with another soda.

"ALLIGATORS," SAYS THE WEE, POINTING AT THE ALLIGA-tors. The boys and I are again in North America; my wife has gone back to Africa to retrieve the diaper bag, which contains, we hope, the car keys. "They got feet and toes like me. Like under my socks." I tell The Wee that's so. I tell The Toad to stop climbing the rail separating him from the alligators. He's breaking his own rule, I say. In the interest of general safety, we head for the gift shop. All trips to the zoo, it seems, bend toward the gift shop. "You can get whatever you want," The Toad tells me. "You can get a kid toy, or a grown-up fragile thing." I thank him for his generosity.

The Toad selects a zoo truck, and The Wee chooses a green monkey with Velcro hands. These they happily play with out in the sun until their mother returns from the tram — is all the world just one big shuttle ride from one grown-up fragile thing to the next? — triumphant, carrying the diaper bag, keys within. "I liked the water-birds the best," The Toad is telling his brother. "They

go on water motorcycles and even their outside stuff is underwater, like their house and their stuff, and —"
He looks up. "Daddy," he says, "what kinds of stuff do birds have?"

I tell him I don't know. He thinks I know everything; I've told him there are seven things I don't know, and now I tell him that this is one of them. He regards me with suspicion, but then ducks back into his own world, a kid's world, a world where it makes as much sense as anything else for giraffes and ostriches to come walking by. A world where there might be soda. Where his mom always finds the keys. Where, if we're lucky, there's always a gift shop at the end. *Os*

NC Zoo

• ASHEBORO •

One of the largest natural-habitat zoos in the country, the North Carolina Zoo forgoes concrete enclosures in favor of trees, ponds, grass, and dirt, and features animals from Africa and North America. Bonus: Just about anyone can take a day trip to the zoo, as it's located near the center of the state. For more information, call (800) 488-0444, or visit nczoo.org.

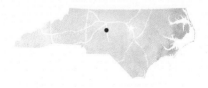

Did you know? That measuring tool is a Brannock Device. The Toad tries it out and learns that he has wide feet.

A PROPER
PAIR OF SHOES

Finding new kicks and nostalgia in Reidsville.

The Toad needs shoes. I head to the local outpost of a discount shoe chain. The shoes cost one million

dollars, even discounted. I try a big-box retailer, which is horrifying, but the shoes only cost $20. "Only." Ha. They begin self-destructing in the car on the way home. At dinner one night that week, I deliver a set of prepared remarks on the cost of shoes; on the general lack of quality products these days; on how when I was a kid, soda cost 30 cents; and you kids get off my lawn. No one really listens to me until I say that what we need is an actual shoe store. A real one. Like from when we were kids.

The Toad locks right in. "Can we buy roller skates?" he asks.

His mom tells him that second grade is probably a better time for roller skates. He's only 5. The Toad throws himself onto the floor in protest. The bottom falls off his left shoe.

"Don't you remember?" I ask my wife. The guy measures your foot, he disappears into the back, tells you he's out of stock in *that* one, but why not try *this* on for size? And in your new sneakers, straightaway you can run faster and jump higher. You wear those suckers out of the store, and your feet *glow*. Your mother yells at you to be careful. To try not to scuff them up. You get an Orange Julius in the food court, and then you go home. It's the best. I *loved* the shoe store.

My wife points to The Toad, still face-down on the floor. She says, "You want to take that to a real store? Go right ahead."

There's only one hitch: Like record stores and Sprite in those green, bumpy bottles, real shoe stores are hard to come by these days. But I find one, I think, in Reidsville. I call to make sure they're the real deal. "We measure the feet of every person who comes in here," the man says, in a tone equal parts suspicious of and sorry for me. I tell him we'll be there in an hour.

I WANT TO TELL YOU ABOUT U.S. HIGHWAY 29 OUT OF Greensboro. How I've always had a little love affair with it. How almost right away, you feel like you're out of the city. How five or 10 miles north, you could once find Green's Supper Club, where my grad-school landlord used to take us for ice-cold beers on the way back from minor league baseball games in Danville and Martinsville, just over the Virginia state line. But Reidsville's only a few exits up. Look: We're already at the Pennrose Mall, already at Strader's Shoe Store.

Motto: "Better Shoes for all the Family."

Sam Lindsey, who now owns Strader's, has been with the store for more than 40 years. He's a big man with a giant handshake, and he knows right away who his customer is. He folds himself down to The Toad's height. He produces the foot-measuring tool. The Toad asks if it will hurt. "Oh, no," Lindsey says. We discover that The Toad has a wide foot. The Toad wants to know if *that* will hurt, having a wide foot. "It's perfect for climbing trees and waterskiing," Lindsey tells him, and heads for the back.

We do not choose the shoes. Sam Lindsey returns with what he thinks might do the trick, a pair of bright red and neon green sneakers that look like a mash-up between a track shoe and a monster truck tire. They're unrepentantly ugly. The Toad loves them. "They're fast, now," Lindsey warns him. "You gotta be careful, they're so fast."

We've gone back in time, is the thing. Lindsey knows the first and last names of every single person who comes in the store while we're there. It's all smiles and jokes and *how's your mom doing?*

LATER, WE SPEND THE AFTERNOON IN DOWNTOWN Reidsville. We walk the tree-lined streets and split a Play-Dough milkshake, an electric-yellow vanilla-and-cookie-dough concoction from the Downtown Dog House. We check items off of a city-sanctioned scavenger hunt: the green city seal, an orange hand, "cats numbering two." The Toad sits on the steps of the granite-columned police station, keeps checking out his new kicks, and allows that he's had a pretty good day.

But what I keep going back to is that mall, and The Toad picking his wide foot up about as high as his ear, then slamming it down onto the polished concrete floor. "Look how loud I can stomp now!" he hollers, his words echoing. Inside Strader's, Sam Lindsey has moved on to another customer, another kid about The Toad's age. You stand there, and you wonder how long a thing like a shoe store might hang on. How long shoe stores might last. And you hope, if you're me — your kid in his new shoes, running through a sun-soaked atrium and climbing up on a coin-operated fighter jet straight from your own childhood — that the answer is a long, long time yet. *Os*

Strader's Shoe Store

· REIDSVILLE ·

Strader's has been in business since 1932, so they know what it means to find the perfect fit. Once you've picked up a new pair of kicks, head downtown to the playground at Courtland Park for a test run, or explore the nature trails around Lake Reidsville. For more information, call (336) 349-5659, or visit stradershoes.com.

ON CAVES & COPPERHEADS

Hibernating doesn't always mean staying home. Sometimes, it means ending a cold, wet day with much-needed hospitality. And cobbler.

Sometimes it rains on your family hike, and that's OK. Just visualize a cozy spot at the end of the trek.

Winter. Rain for a week. Seven or eight degrees colder and we'd have snow, but no. It's our second consecutive shut-in Saturday morning. There is not, and could not be, enough coffee. The kids are bonkers, taking laps through the house. They'd be knocking priceless heirlooms to the ground if we had any. What does get knocked to the ground: a full bowl of Rice Krispies, milk and all. "That's it," I say.

"We have to get out."

"But it's raining," the kids say.

"Yes," I say. "But rain or no, mud or no, hypothermia or no, we have to get out. Where do you want to go?"

The Toad says: "To the cave. Let's go to that cave."

"What cave?" I ask.

"The one with the snake," he says.

"Great," I say. "Let's go."

What he means is Boone's Cave Park, just outside of Lexington, which our family calls Copperhead State Park. Here is the delightful reason why: The last time we were there, The Toad found a copperhead. Full-size. Between his feet. He and I were walking along, speaking as men speak, when he stopped dead in the trail and began to scream. No words. Just screaming.

"What did I see? What did I see?" he asked me, after he got his words back, after he and I had all but levitated back down the trail. Regarding adrenaline: Had you needed anything seen, heard, or smelled within a radius of 50 miles just then, I'd have been your man. I worked, rapid-fire, through several sucking-the-venom-out scenarios. Boy Scout tourniquets. That kind of thing. "A snake," I told him. "You saw a snake. You did just right. Don't ever tell your mom."

Though we did tell his mom: We were outside, and outside is where snakes tend to live, so by the transitive property of parenting, I'd done nothing wrong. She mentions the copperhead today, though, as she declines our invitation to go back to the cave. "Snakes hibernate," I tell her, which I'm pretty sure is true. Still, she says, she's not going; a cold weather hike is not really her thing. "Be careful," she tells us. "Don't worry," I say. The boys and I layer up and head out.

THE CAVE, WHERE LEGEND HOLDS THAT A YOUNG Daniel Boone hung out, is at the bottom of a not-terribly-long trail, and down several hundred wooden steps. It's almost hilariously small if you're an adult-size person, but it's pretty cave-like if you're not. It also turns out to be a solid place for persons of all sizes to wait out a torrentially rainy half-hour.

Here are some questions for a long winter's night: If two boys continually slip and fall in the winter-slick forest, and only their father is around to hear, then what is the sound of one hand clapping? What's the remedy for first one child, and then the other, bumping his head on the roof of Daniel Boone's alleged cave? How miserable do you have to be before you give up?

Don't answer that last one. Just go ahead and give up. And let me recommend, once you've slogged back up the trail and toweled off, landing at the counter at Lexington Barbecue. It's a huge white barn made famous by its excellent barbecue, as well as glowing write-ups in various magazines, but that's not what we're on about here.

What I want to say is this: Should you find yourself the bone-cold father of two bone-cold boys, and should you extract yourself, largely unhurt, from bone-cold Copperhead State Park, there's only one thing better than introducing those boys to their first cobbler. It's seeing the waitress clock the various missteps you've made in your day and week and, give or take, the past five years. It's seeing her take your kids into her confidence and telling them no, they don't have to choose between cherry and peach. It's watching two obscenely large half-and-half cobblers come out of the kitchen and then make it partly into, but mainly onto, your children. It's the stack of napkins and the cup of coffee the waitress brings without your having to ask. It's your glasses steaming up and your sons on either side of you, breathless from the heat and the sugar and the press of winter, and what you want to say is, "Boys, this is what a cave is, this is hibernation," but you don't, because for one thing, that doesn't make any sense, and then also sometimes, sometimes you manage to keep your mouth shut and just let things be. **O𝔰**

Boone's Cave Park

· DAVIDSON COUNTY ·

In addition to the small cave thought to have been Daniel Boone's hideout, this 110-acre park offers several trails, a picnic area, a 1700s-style cabin, campsites, and access to the Yadkin River. For more information, call (336) 242-2285, or visit visitdavidsoncounty.com.

ALL NOISE,
ALL THE TIME

Seeking an echo in Nantahala National Forest.

The Toad
demonstrates
an echo. Step 1:
Yell loudly. Step
2: Listen quietly.
The second step
is always harder.

We find the camp store in the Standing Indian Campground in the Nantahala National Forest

by complete, almost farcical, accident. We find it by way of a small brown roadside sign, the kind with a picnic table and a tent on it, the sort of sign that suggests there might be something down the road a bit. We are in search of a ravine, because we are in search of an echo, and the road twists so steeply and suddenly down into nothing that it feels like we must be on the right track. (We are also in search of that picnic table, or at least a spot free from poison ivy and marauding forest creatures, because it is past the kids' lunchtimes and they are acting like it, smacking each other with Legos in the back seat; it is past our lunchtimes, too, and my wife and I are acting like it, give or take smacking each other with Legos in the front seat.)

It takes six years to find the bottom of the road. By the end of those six years, I have aged 10. Still: picnic tables. Hiking trails. Running water, even, and a country store, like a mirage, with rocking chairs on a tiny front porch. Inside, along with a lone loaf of Wonder Bread and a couple of bags of Doritos and a half-dozen walking sticks, sits an old-school lowboy ice-cream cooler containing ice-cream sandwiches and Klondike bars and Push-up Pops. I've gone in to case the joint, and to pay the $2 daily-use fee for the campground. I come back bearing good news: If everyone can use good manners, then we can hike a trail that chases along the headwaters of the Nantahala River. And there is ice cream.

Which means, obviously, that we eat our ice cream before we eat our lunch, which means that nobody gets much actual lunch in them, but I take the rare opportunity not to freak out about this, and therefore we keep the peace. High-fructose corn syrup: the salve that heals most wounds.

WHY AN ECHO? YOU MAY BE ASKING. BECAUSE ECHOES are cool. They just are. They are also quite difficult to explain. "You mean the thing that makes your voice louder?" The Toad asked, when it first came up. He's at the age where he can ask questions for days. "The thing in the ceiling?" Sort of, I said. Then he went from room to room, shouting, "THIS. IS. AN. ECHO." But it was not. So: road trip.

We hike. We peel off our socks and shoes and stand, at 3,800 feet above sea level, in the shallow, chilly Nantahala. The Wee looks down at all the water, and starts yelling "AGUA! AGUA!" He's telling us about it, and it seems not to make any difference how many times we agree that it's there. The Toad, armed with a stick, spends the bulk of our afternoon walk pushing the stick into the various springs and rivulets that cross the trail in search of "kickstand," by which he means quicksand. He takes the fact that he doesn't find any pretty well. And I am not so much disappointed not to find an echo — on the Park Creek Trail, I do not think it is possible for a person who wishes to be outside to be disappointed — as I am chagrined. What we needed, of course, was some kind of rock canyon. Not a bubbling brook.

I apologize for my child, who is now standing dead center in the road, screaming out his name.

The Toad tries for an echo at the end of the day, back at the country store, and gets maybe half of one, or half the idea. I apologize to the woman running the counter, and to the folks overnighting in the campground, for my child, who is now standing dead center in the road, screaming out his name — and for his brother, who is joining in, ever eager to be big. We buy another round of ice cream, mainly to quiet them. Both boys are dead asleep by the time we crawl the several miles back to the main road.

THAT WEEKEND, BACK HOME, MY PHONE RINGS. IT'S MY wife; she's taken The Toad to the library to borrow books about vehicles. "Guess where we are," she says, and I say something about how I was hoping it would be the library. "In the parking garage," she says. "In the stairwell." By which she means the three-story glass-and-steel-and-concrete stairwell, and she says, "I'll hold the phone out," and she does, and what I hear is The Toad, saying, "Wait. Whoops! There's an echo in here!" He says it over and over, and the stairwell says it back to him. He comes home delighted: They found a book on fast trains and faster jets. "Plus, Daddy," he says, almost whispering, taking me into his confidence, "my voice is in the stairs."

And in the Nantahala, buddy, and everywhere else. You and your brother both. You guys are all noise, except for when you're not. Just hang on a second — let's listen. Let's see what we might hear. *O8*

Standing Indian Campground

· FRANKLIN ·

Standing Indian Campground is a great home base for exploring the surrounding forest, and provides access to hiking trails and the Nantahala River. Explore for the day and make use of the general store and picnic area for lunch, or stick around and use the campsites. For more information, call (828) 524-6441, or visit recreation.gov.

LOST IN STOKES COUNTY

Leave the map behind: Navigating uncharted territory is good for the soul.

Getting lost on purpose is like riding a merry-go-round — scary at first, but mostly just fun.

Our aim was to get lost, and we did. I left without a paper map, and although I had my phone, and could have figured out how to make it yell at me to turn left, then right, where's the fun in that? The phone rode in the glove compartment.

Twenty miles in, a whimper from the back seat: The Toad. "What's up, kiddo?" I asked him.

"Azulito is scared," he said. His bear. Blue. Six inches tall. "She doesn't want to be lost."

"Tell her not to worry," I said.

"Daddy," said The Wee. "Azulito is scary."

"Gentlemen," I told them, "we'll be fine."

We were aiming for the town of Belews Creek, because a little pre-trip research suggested it might be on a body of water not far from home. We never found it. Even though there were signs, and a Belews Creek Road. What we did find: that the land rises up off the Piedmont much more suddenly than I'd ever realized. "It's the mountains!" The Wee said, and I was agreeing with him for sport, but then, there, out the passenger window, was Pilot Mountain, and all manner of other hills. It's gorgeous country out that way, and we traced highway to wooded highway until we really were lost, until I said so, until The Toad was asking if he could please say a curse word now, until we landed in Walnut Cove.

I stopped at a diner on Main Street — the Main Street Diner — where, in the window, somebody'd hung a flyer advertising baby hedgehogs for sale. "Daddy," The Toad said. "If we're lost, does that mean we left the earth?"

I told him I thought not.

He said, "But are we even on the same planet anymore?"

"In the best way," I told him.

We emerged from the diner not with hedgehogs but with PB&Js wrapped in white paper, crossed the street, and ate in a little park that fronts the Walnut Cove Public Library. When we finished, we skulked around the Walnut Cove Volunteer Fire & Rescue department, home of many shiny trucks. Then, the kids wanted a playground. I asked inside the diner about such a thing. I got directions I pretended to understand, complete with this: "Now, if you hit the Shell station up there, you've gone too far."

NORTH CAROLINA WATER COUNTRY — RIVER AND LAKE country, anyway — is all boat launches and fresh eggs and Kountry Korner groceries and taxidermy shops, and that's what we drove through until we found Germanton Park, which has not just a playground, but a playground from my youth, the type so excellent and dangerous that it's hard to imagine how it's survived litigation. There are seesaws made from 20-foot wooden beams. There's a huge metal slide. There are whirling metal jungle-gym-type things, which The Toad kept calling roundabouts, though I don't think that's what they're called, and I was immediately spinning the boys ever faster, ever closer to something bound to look like a spiral fracture if either of them were to hazard a dismount. I have pictures on that needless phone; I wish, so very much, that I had sound.

I used to do this more: set out looking to get lost. There's not nearly enough of it these days. Not enough danger, either, at least not of the immediate, corporeal sort: The Wee, who for months has refused to wear any pants other than the short variety, tore up his knee on the wooden castle that led to the slide. Here's how long he was sad: long enough for me to explain that if he'd just wear a pair of jeans, this type of thing wouldn't happen. Long enough for me to undo my own argument about danger. He looked me in the eye, made a clear calculation — *this skinned knee seems a fair trade* — and went on playing. They both did. For far longer than I meant to stay. But how can you pull kids away from a real playground? How hard must you work not to run over there, not to stop them from getting on the seesaw, not to explain that what goes up must come, often suddenly, back down?

You try your best — that's the thing. It's all you can do. Let them learn what getting lost teaches you. What uncharted territory really is. Your father can tell you things again and again, I now well know, but you never believe until you see it, or feel it, for yourself. ❧

Germanton Park

• GERMANTON •

Germanton Park includes swings, play equipment, walking trails, picnic shelters, and volleyball courts. It also features adaptive playground equipment for uniquely-abled children, making the park particularly inclusive. For more information, call (336) 413-5321.

THE EDGE OF SUMMER

*Friends and family and long, lazy days on the lake:
This is almost-summer in North Carolina.*

If you're not ready to
jump in, a dock is just
as good a place for
contemplating the lake
and soaking up the sun.

There they are, at the end of the dock: The Toad and The Wee. Their backs are to us. They're looking down.

Moments like this can land with a kind of physical force: The boys exist. It's not that I ever forget, but then something stills, slows, and I'm reminded. There they are.

Let's put those boys in life jackets just slightly too large for them. Let's stand them out on the edge of the dock. Below, already in the water: the older boys, the children of these other two couples who have let us so fully into their lives. Their boys have already learned to brave the jump. They are boys one full turn of the wheel in front of ours. They are boys whose old clothes our boys wear. Side benefit of having best friends whose children grow out of their clothes just as yours grow in: Well, that *is* the side benefit.

They taught us how to do this, these two couples. Let us come to their houses with our infant son, told us things would be mainly OK. Let us bring the second baby over, told us we may have thought we were tired before, but that we'd learn to survive. Our first child once fell asleep on a dog bed at a dinner party at one couple's house. Our second concusses himself regularly in the other couple's tree house. We all live half a block apart. Summer cookouts. Winter stews. How it goes: Feed the kids and prop them up in front of a movie, open another bottle of wine. Sit inside by the fire or outside under string lights and tell each other, in so many words, that we love each other.

ONE OF THE COUPLES HAS A LAKE HOUSE, HAS INVITED us again and again, and again and again we've said no, not this year, our kids are too little, all of it code for: We can pull it together enough to see you in the neighborhood, but we're such a traveling circus that we'll wait till the boys are older. Except then they get older. So the next time, we say yes, what can we bring, see you tomorrow, and we pack the 400 things it takes for us to leave the house for a period longer than 30 minutes, and we go. It's a Saturday drive through a part of North Carolina that gets not nearly enough press — neither mountains nor sea, south and west on two-lane highways toward Lake Norman, past fields and hills and forests and almost liquid sunshine and the still-new green of that hinterland between spring and summer.

The little one will cry that night from 2 to 3 a.m. The big one will steal — out and out *steal* — a Hot Wheels motorcycle the next day, and will have to be marched down the street to apologize when we get home. But none of that is now. Now is the dock, the boat traffic back and forth out in the channel, the cove swallowing echoes, the adults in Adirondack chairs and the big boys paddling kayaks and my boys standing, considering.

Our friends have pictures framed in their hallways: kids suspended midair, mid-flight, headed down into lake water. Holding hands, even. When I realize that that's what I'm hoping for, I put the camera down, slip off my sandals, peel off most of my clothes, and climb down the ladder. *Come on in*, I tell them, and they stare down. A truth: It will be tomorrow before The Toad jumps, and The Wee won't jump at all this year. For now, they climb down the ladder one slippery rung at a time, the prospect of that plenty daunting

They are baptized in the murky lake, and soon enough they're each cutting loose from me.

enough. But they do it, friends: They are baptized in the murky lake, and soon enough they're each cutting loose from me, swimming, playing with the idea of floating, with the idea of being near me but not really needing me, not right away.

Later on, we'll all have dinner on the huge screened-in porch, a storm off in the distance rumbling away, somebody across the lake shooting mid-grade fireworks.

The adults — well, one of us will catch another's eye while the kids are eating, while there's a moment of quiet brought on by hot dogs and the kind of tired only swimming brings, and it's not hard to imagine what won't get said, but what gets said just as surely, all the same: *Thanks for the life jackets. For this cold beer. For your children, patient with mine. For the wild miracle of living just down the street. For inviting us to this plain, perfect house. To this place. We're so tired. We're so lucky. Let's do it all over again in the morning.* **Os**

Lake Norman State Park

• TROUTMAN •

Less than an hour's drive from Uptown Charlotte, Lake Norman State Park offers a beach, a boat ramp, extensive trails for walking, and a family campground. For swimming and more, head to the largest man-made lake in the state. For more information, call (704) 528-6350, or visit ncparks.gov.

THE PROMISE OF A PEACH

How can such a simple summertime pleasure say so much about the history of the Sandhills, and tradition, and being happy with what you've got?

They might be young, but The Wee (left) and The Toad already know that summer has a taste: peaches from Candor.

Headed south on U.S. Highway 220, just past Seagrove and pottery country, there is an exit for

the communities of Ether and Steeds. The sign reads: Ether Steeds. The names are one atop the other, but still, one can't help but think: great name for an antihero in some novel, a guy with a loyal dog, an ex-wife he still hopes to win back, and some kind of mild gambling habit. Maybe he bets on the high school tennis team. Maybe he's also trying to build a submarine in his backyard. He makes a handful of grand gestures. High jinks ensue. He walks a tightrope between making it and not.

Letting this plan buzz through my head is how I miss the exit for Candor, and for Johnson's Peaches.

But the kids holler and my wife hollers and I am called back to my regularly scheduled life, and we turn the car around to make good on a yearly promise: Yes, children of mine, boys of this plain, happily stable marriage, you may stand at the farmers market or a produce stand or, in this case, at the mother ship itself, the parking lot of

Johnson's Peaches, and you may eat a peach as if it were an apple. You may let the juice run down your chin and down your forearms. We will towel you off afterward, and then we can buy a whole peck of peaches and be on our way.

OF ALL THE RITES OF SUMMER, THE BOYS EATING peaches is maybe my favorite. Johnson's, like any operation worth the paint on its sign, has it wired pretty well: The peaches for sale in the baskets aren't fully ripe yet (so that you can get them home unbruised), but back behind the counter tend to be several perfectly ripe peaches, possibly of the scratch-and-dent variety, but still tailor-made for a kid needing instant gratification. Or his dad. What says summer more than a peach? What's more decadent? How better to let a child in on one of the sharpest wonders of the world? Here, you say. Eat this. Tell me anything that's better.

Johnson's, the largest grower in the area, sells more than 50 varieties of peaches over the course of the season. I ask Mrs. Johnson — nobody seems to use her first name, though I later find out that it's Barbara — which her favorite is. "The one that makes the most money," she says, half-letting me in on half a joke. It's not an easy life, she says: Back when she and her husband took over the business from his father (who planted the original orchards around 1930), "we worked day and night to keep the operation going." She tells me there aren't that many growers left. "Take Miss Peach," she says. "Used to be a great competition. Now somebody just chooses somebody they know in the peach business."

Johnson's is the only thing at the exit — the only thing I can see, anyway. White building, red roof, gravel parking lot. Peaches upon peaches. My kids care not much yet for the great sweep of history, for the saga of a region told in blossom and yield and the price

How better to let a child in on one of the sharpest wonders of the world? Here, you say. Eat this. Tell me anything that's better.

of a tractor. They don't know — and, come on, neither do I — what it takes to make a thing like Johnson's go. They're starting to learn, though, the difference between a real peach and a grocery-store peach, and what we're working on, my wife and I, is teaching them about the growing season, about where things come from, about how many people work dawn to dusk to build the world around them. Yet we're also trying to keep them from some of that — to let them just have the pure joy that is a single peach, and not have to worry themselves too much with the rough-and-tumble outside world.

The boys finish up, wiping their mouths on their

hands and their arms and the hems of their shirts before we can get to them with our thousand napkins. Let Ether Steeds concern himself with spelling out his beloved's name in burning lighter fluid on the football field, I'm thinking. Let the truly crazy stuff play out somewhere else. I'll take — every day — this plainer life, my wife, these boys, these endless tiny joys. We take the children one at a time to the water fountain, all but hose them off. Can we have another peach? they want to know, once they're clean. Sure, we tell them, sure, and we start all over again. *Os*

Johnson's Peaches

• CANDOR •

Since 1934, the Johnsons have been growing peaches on their family farm. At their market, you'll find all the peaches you could dream of, along with nectarines, plums, apples, and pears. For the sweetest of sweet tooths, the Johnsons also sell homemade peach ice cream, peach dumplings, and more. For more information, call (910) 974-7730, or visit johnsonspeaches.com.

Drew and his wife, Tita Ramirez, are teaching The Wee (left) and The Toad what it means to be a North Carolinian.

Drew Perry is the author of the novels This Is Just Exactly Like You, *a finalist for the Flaherty-Dunnan First Novel Prize from the Center for Fiction, and* Kids These Days, *an Amazon Best-of-the-Month pick. He is a frequent contributor to* Our State, *seeking danger at every turn — whether in a hot air balloon, aboard an RV on two-lane mountain roads, or chasing his two young boys through "Family Tradition" columns from the headwaters of the Nantahala to the Intracoastal Waterway. He and his family live in Greensboro, and he has taught writing at Elon University since 1999.*